TABLE OF CONTENTS

LIST OF ACRONYMS AND ABBREVIATIONS

BTS	Base Transceiver Station
CSIS	Canadian Security Intelligence Service
FDI	Foreign Direct Investment
IME	Institute of Microelectronics
IP DSLAM	Internet Protocol Digital Subscriber Line Access Multiplexer
LTE	Long-term Evolution
MIMO	Multi-input Multi-output
NGN	Next Generation Networking
OAS	Organization of American States
PBX	Private Branch Exchange
PLA	People's Liberation Army
UMTS	Universal Mobile Telecommunications Systems

ACKNOWLEDGMENTS

I would sincerely like to thank Wade Huntley and Linda Kalister for their guidance during the writing of this thesis. I met unexpected challenges during the process, and Wade and Linda helped with their ideas and encouragement.

I would also like to acknowledge my professors at the Naval Postgraduate School, who assisted in my understanding of both Latin American security, as well as cyber technologies.

I would like to thank my loving family for their continued support through all that I do. Any success that I have in my career I owe to them.

I. THE LONG-TERM U.S. STRATEGIC IMPLICATIONS OF HUAWEI'S PENETRATION IN LATIN AMERICA

A. MAJOR RESEARCH QUESTION

One of the most important concerns of any nation is security. A nation's security can be threatened in many ways by many different adversaries. This thesis will address one simple example of a security threat. What are the long-term strategic implications of Chinese telecommunications penetration into Latin America? While there are multiple examples of Chinese companies, this case study will focus on Huawei Technologies Incorporated.

B. IMPORTANCE

The importance of this work can be illustrated by addressing two framing questions. First, why should the U.S. care about Latin America? Second, why should the U.S. care about Huawei's activities? This section addresses these questions, in the latter case through a summary of both Huawei's historical development and its technology.

1. U.S. in Latin America

First, Latin America is close to the United States, geographically. The U.S. is obviously physically bordered by Mexico and only a short trip away from the rest of Latin America. Therefore, any security threat to Latin America presents a potential threat to the U.S. as well, based simply on proximity.

Second, the U.S. also has a close economic relationship with many countries in Latin America.

1

Therefore, any relationship that strongly affects the economics of the region, also impacts the United States.

Finally, the U.S. also considers many Latin American countries to be allies. Not only are these countries allies, but the U.S. even maintains military bases in some of these countries. Anytime there is a strong foreign influence in a country that the U.S. has a presence in, it should be an important matter to officials.

Second, the U.S. also has a close economic relationship with many countries in Latin America. Therefore, any relationship which strongly affects the economics of the region, also impacts the United States.

Finally, the U.S. also considers many Latin American countries to be allies. Not only are these countries allies, but the U.S. even maintains military bases in some of these countries. Anytime there is a strong foreign influence in a country that the U.S. has a presence in, it should be an important matter to officials.

2. Huawei History

For the subsequent analysis, it is necessary to understand Huawei. One of the best ways to fully understand a company is to understand its history. Huawei was established in 1987. This means it was formed during the early generation of post-1978 Chinese companies established after Deng Xiaoping's open-door policy (Shao 2012, para. 7). For more than twenty-five years, Huawei has continued to expand, transforming into the global powerhouse that it is today.

However, Huawei did not begin with this type of strength. "Huawei people, both managers and employees, used to work in a small office that also served as kitchen and dormitory" (Shao 2012, para. 8). This shows Huawei's will for success. It takes great desire to persist through the tough beginnings and create the empire that is Huawei today.

One of the most important aspects of the early stages of Huawei was its business relationships. "Huawei's business partner produced private branch exchange (PBX) switches as their main product offering" (Discovering Huawei's History 2012, under "A Historical Insight"). This partnership would be an important aspect of Huawei's history. After Huawei gained sufficient knowledge on the PBX business, it made a groundbreaking entrance into the mainstream telecommunications market in 1992, launching the C&C08 digital telephone switch (Discovering Huawei's History 2012, under "A Historical Insight"). This was the beginning of one of the most powerful telecommunications companies in the world.

Much of this success must be credited to founder and president Ren Zhengfei. A former member of the People's Liberation Army Engineering Corps, Ren founded Huawei in 1987 (Ren Zhengfei 2012, para. 1). "In 1997, Ren visited a few U.S. multinational corporations, including IBM. He later on mentioned his sentiment of the huge gaps between Chinese and Western companies" (Shao 2012, para. 9). In 1997, China could simply not compete with the U.S. in the technological field. However, this trip would prove extremely valuable for Ren.

Ren knew that change was necessary, and he did everything he could to match U.S. companies. "It engaged IBM, at a substantial cost, to be its technology-training provider. In total, Huawei spent over US$150 million on its transition" (Shao 2012, para. 11). This is a huge commitment from a company with limited success at the time. Luckily for Ren, this investment has easily paid for itself over the years, as Huawei is now a model for success.

3. Huawei Technology

In order to truly understand the power of Huawei, it is important to take a closer look at the current technologies it manufactures. "The company is now a $32billion business empire with 140,000 employees, and customers in 140 countries. It commands respect by delivering high-quality telecoms equipment at low prices" ("Who's Afraid of Huawei?" 2012, para. 2). Huawei's ability to provide this high-end equipment at low prices is one of the biggest reasons it has been so successful in its global expansion.

In addition, Huawei is also a mass producer of infrastructure. "Huawei's sales have surpassed Ericsson's, making the privately held company the largest telco infrastructure maker in the world" (Fitchard 2012, para. 1). Its ability to produce infrastructure worldwide is one of Huawei's biggest strengths.

Huawei's primary business is selling high-end computer networking switches and other equipment used by cellphone carriers, Internet service providers, and other companies to run communications networks (Simonite 2012, para. 1). The purchases from these types of companies, in addition to the multitude of personal devices purchased from Huawei, is a major reason for its success.

One of the most important technological fields today is "big data." "In simplest terms, the phrase refers to the tools, processes and procedures allowing an organization to create, manipulate, and manage very large data sets and storage facilities" (Kusnetzky 2010, para. 3). Huawei is making significant progress in this field.

"Huawei has added 1,000 research and development staff to bolster its storage team, Jiang said. Meanwhile, the company said a public cloud offering is currently in the works" (Hoffman 2012, para. 6). This shows Huawei's significant commitment to cloud computing and its associated technologies. Cloud storage appears to be the way ahead in data-storage technology, and it is a must for any successful data-storage company.

One of the newest Huawei products is Magnum. "Magnum is a cloud-based integrated OSS/BSS system consisting of a software platform and customer service functionalities (including implementation and technical service)" (Morrison and Romaniuk n.d., under "Magnum OSS/BSS-The sweet taste of success"). This cloud-based system is one that Huawei hopes will assist in continuing its expansion in the global market.

Huawei has also created what it calls the Noah's Ark Lab. Huawei's "mission is to conduct the state of the art research on data mining and artificial intelligence by exploring theories and building intelligent systems" (Noah's Ark Lab n.d., para. 1). This research lab is Huawei's means to help ensure that it remains one of the top companies in of the world of technology.

Not only does Huawei offer cloud computing, it offers a mobile cloud as well. "Cloud$^+$ offers a range of next generation features like Cloud$^+$ drive, Message$^+$, Streams, Phone finder, SNS, Contacts Integration and any where any device access for content saved on drive" (Cloud+ n.d., para. 1). As the leading telecommunications company in the world, this technology is an important advancement.

Finally, Huawei is currently pushing OceanStor HVS. "Huawei's HVS series uses Smart Matrix Architecture, and is equipped with XVE, a virtualized storage operating system dedicated to high-end storage systems" ("Huawei Cloud Congress 2012 Shows How Enterprises Can 'Make IT Simple, Make Business Agile' in the Cloud Era" 2012, para. 1). This is one of the most advanced storage systems available on the market today, showing Huawei is at the top of its field.

In addition to advances in big data, Huawei has made great improvements in the mobile phone field. Huawei's mobile-chip company, MediaTek, recently "launched the world's first quad-core 'system on a chip' for smartphones. The new chip, the MT6589, is cheaper to manufacture—which will help lower the price of smartphone hardware globally" (Muncaster 2012, para. 1). If the price of these smartphones decreases, they will become increasingly popular worldwide, especially in the poorer countries in Latin America, where they are not as easily affordable. This growth would give Huawei even more power in the region.

Huawei has only recently entered the field of smartphone production. "In 2012, Huawei has shipped 85 percent of its devices under its own brand, compared to a scant 20 percent in 2011" (Dillet 2013, para. 1). This sharp increase shows the potential for Huawei's dominance in mobile devices. "Chief Marketing Officer Shao Yang declared to Le Monde that the company plans to become one of the top 5 smartphone brands in 2014 and one of the top 3 in 2016" (Dillet 2013, para. 2).

While this seemed like a reasonable goal, Huawei has already exceeded these expectations, becoming the number three smartphone producer in the fourth quarter of 2012. "In 2012 overall, Huawei sold 27.2 million smartphones, up 73.8 percent from the year before" (Albanesius 2013, para. 2).

Huawei has recently launched its first smartphone available to U.S. consumers, the Ascend P1. "The Android-powered device is equipped with a 4.3-inch Super AMOLED display, a 1.5GHz dual-core processor, 1GB of RAM and an 8-megapixel rear camera" (Graziano 2013, para. 1). This technologically advanced smartphone is available easily through Amazon or Best Buy. While this was the first Huawei mobile device available in the U.S., there are already more available in stores. This is a clear example of Huawei's expansion into the United States.

One of the key advantages that Huawei has over other companies lies in the production. "Huawei manufactures its own phones. Apple, Nokia, HTC, Motorola and others rely on third-party manufacturers like [Taiwan Manufacturer] Foxconn, which increases costs and reduces flexibility"

7

(Dillet 2013, para. 5). This advantage of not having to rely on a third-party manufacturer makes Huawei's success even more probable.

It is clear from all of these technological advancements that Huawei is a formidable telecommunications company. Examples of this are its big data technologies and advanced smartphones. These products have allowed Huawei to expand all over the globe, gaining power as it grows. One of the regions into which Huawei has expanded is Latin America. This expansion has potential strategic implications for the United States, which shall be evaluated at this time.

C.   PROBLEMS AND HYPOTHESIS

In presenting this thesis, multiple problems came about. The first problem was trying to get a solid grasp and understanding of Huawei Technologies. Huawei has historically been a relatively opaque company. It has recently been more open to the public, but its ownership structure remains clouded.

Second, is the problem of establishing both U.S. and Chinese interests in Latin America. In order to show the relevance of this thesis, it is important to show that not only is China interested in expanding in Latin America, but also, the United States cares about this expansion. Once this is established, it is clearer whether Huawei's expansion affects the U.S. or not.

The third problem is that of separating suspicions and evidence. Notably, there is less proof of Huawei posing a security threat than there are published suspicions. In order to properly identify the security threat of Huawei, it is necessary to show what evidence is presented and what evidence is missing.

These problems are addressed in this thesis, making it clearer as to what type of threat Huawei's expansion into Latin America poses to the United States. The author finds positive support for the hypothesis that there is a significant security threat to both proprietary information and compromised communications equipment, presented even by the limited evidence against Huawei currently available, and that the U.S. should take action to limit Huawei's expansion while also seeking further evidence to evaluate less substantiated claims.

D.   THESIS OVERVIEW

This first chapter of this thesis has introduced the idea of Huawei's expansion into Latin America. It has highlighted the importance of this topic with a summary description of U.S. Latin American interests, and by examining the background of Huawei. In order to do this properly, both the history of Huawei and its current available technologies were reviewed. This review has shown that Huawei Technologies Inc. is a Chinese telecommunications company that is making tremendous economic gains worldwide.

With this understanding of Huawei's background, the next two chapters evaluate the strategic implications of its penetration into Latin America. The second chapter focuses on the economic impact of Huawei's expansion into Latin America. In order to do this, both Chinese and American interests in Latin America are examined. Next, the chapter describes Huawei's presence, nature of contracts, and economic threat. On this basis, the chapter then evaluates whether Huawei's penetration into Latin America is threatening to U.S. economic interests.

The third chapter focuses on the security concerns that Huawei's expansion poses. These concerns are more difficult to identify. The main reason for this is the lack of solid evidence supporting claims of Huawei's illegal activities. In order to manage this problem, this chapter presents all of the suspicions involving Huawei, and then distinguishes the evidence present to support those suspicions from the evidence that is missing. This evaluation does not absolve Huawei of incrimination where evidence is lacking. Rather, distinguishing concerns that are supported by evidence from those that are not will enable future inquiry to focus on where evidence is needed to validate concerns, supporting more nuanced policy-making.

The fourth and final chapter concludes by summarizing the findings of this thesis in previous chapters. With the economic and security concerns of Huawei's penetration into Latin America identified, the strategic implications for the U.S. can be evaluated. This chapter shows that a clear link can be drawn between Huawei's activity in Latin America and U.S. security. In addition to summarizing the findings, recommendations for both future work and possible actions to be taken against Huawei are presented. The chapter evaluates options that include limiting Huawei's expansion, attaining more evidence to support such decisions, or simply allowing Huawei to continue its current trends. Thesis recommendations are based on the current evidence that is available to the public.

II. THE ECONOMIC IMPACT OF HUAWEI'S EXPANSION IN LATIN AMERICA

A.   U.S. INTERESTS IN LATIN AMERICA

The first way to evaluate the strategic implications of Huawei's expansion into Latin America is through America's economic concerns. In order to properly evaluate these concerns, U.S. economic interests in Latin America must be the first factor highlighted.

The United States is one of the most dominant economic players in Latin America. "U.S. geographic proximity to Latin America, close cultural ties, and long-standing trade patterns give the United States overwhelming advantages" (Engel 2008, para. 11). This shows that Latin America is more than simply a trading ground to the United States. "We share historical, cultural, commercial, even familial ties" (Reich 2002, under "Introduction"). These bonds explain this close relationship that exists in the Western Hemisphere.

One of the biggest reasons for the close relationship is politics. Almost all Latin American countries now have democratic forms of government. The Inter-American Democratic Charter makes the nations of this hemisphere and the Organization of American States (OAS) unique in the world because of our commitment to democracy (Reich 2002, under "Introduction"). This is one of the reasons for U.S. interests in Latin America.

Since eight of the top ten U.S. trade partners have a democratic form of government (Iseman 2012, under table), it is reasonable to assume that the U.S. prefers to trade with nations with democratic governments. Not only does the U.S. prefer to deal with these nations, it wants to support democracy and help maintain internal stability.

Mexico and Central America are examples of regions that depend economically on their exports to the United States more than anything else. This relationship with Mexico is not just one-sided. President George W. Bush was quoted as saying, "there is no relationship the world over that is more relevant to the United States than the one with Mexico" (Crandall and Hunter 2008, 242). This statement clearly recognizes the importance of the U.S. relationship with Mexico.

The United States also maintains very strong relationships in South America. One example of that is the relationship with Chile. "The main concern and orientation of Chile's foreign policy has been toward creating and maintaining ties with the American superpower" (Moronde 2003, 246). Latin American countries, such as Chile, understand the importance of this relationship as much as the United States. In fact, the U.S. sells more to the Southern Cone (Argentina, Chile, Paraguay, and Uruguay) than to China (Reich 2002, under "Introduction").

Even countries that the United States has had strained relationships with in the past still show signs of cooperation. An example of this is Brazil. Arturo Valenzuela, the former U.S. Assistant Secretary of the State for Western Hemisphere Affairs, has stated his desire for a strong relationship with Brazil. Valenzuela claimed the U.S. government will work with American exporters and investors to expand trade in Brazil, and it will devote

12

more resources to efforts that strengthen the bilateral mechanisms with Brazil, such as the Economic Partnership Dialogue (Valenzuela 2011, para. 27). This shows the U.S. commitment to maintaining this relationship with Brazil.

In addition, Brazil also supported the U.S. during its most difficult time. "Brazil was the first country to show solidarity with the United States immediately following the September 11 attacks" (Crandall and Crandall 2008, 159). Brazil was not the only nation to join forces with the U.S. during this trying time. "Thirty-two of the 34 OAS member states have also signed a hemispheric convention against terrorism to enhance regional cooperation in the fight against this scourge" (Reich 2002, under "The War on Terrorism"). These strong relationships that the United States maintains throughout most of Latin America are why it remains a regional power in Western Hemisphere.

Another Latin American country that the U.S. has had a very difficult relationship with is Cuba. However, this relationship has improved recently as well. "During the first two years of the Obama Administration, we have taken measures to increase contact between separated families and to promote the free flow of information to, from, and within Cuba" (Valenzuela 2011, para. 14). This is a huge change from the previous policies of travel restrictions. While the U.S. still opposes the communist government of Cuba, it is clear that it has reduced its tough stance on the country, allowing for a better relationship.

B.   CHINESE ECONOMIC INTERESTS IN LATIN AMERICA

Since World War II, the United States has been one of, if not the only dominant player in Latin American affairs.

It has been argued by some observers that this is no longer the case, and that China has now emerged as a top external economic actor.

In order to determine whether this is true, one must first examine the current relationship between China and Latin America. This will be done by comparing each side's motivations and the challenges faced by both parties. Finally, this relationship must be compared with the longstanding relationship Latin America has had with the United States.

First, one must understand the motivations for the relationship between China and Latin America. "Since April 2000 when President Jiang Zemin became the first Chinese official to visit the region, commercial ties between the two regions broadened and deepened" (Bruno 2012, para. 1). China has multiple reasons for getting involved in the Western Hemisphere. The first, and most obvious, is trade.

One of China's main trade interests in Latin America is commodities. "It has lifted growth for years in commodity producers such as Brazil, Argentina, Chile and Peru with its voracious demand for raw goods such as iron ore, copper, and soy" (Grudgings and Gardner 2011, para. 5). This trade has given these countries a huge economic boost. "Its purchases of commodities and raw materials from the region drive trade surpluses year after year." (Roett and Paz 2008, 14).

While these commodities and raw materials are some of the main reasons for involvement in Latin America, China's interest in oil imports has increased as well. "With Chinese domestic oil production declining, China's

14

dependence on oil imports will inevitably increase" (Roett and Paz 2008, 18). This has become apparent with the evolving relationship between China and Venezuela. Venezuela is a top-fifteen oil-producing country, exporting an estimated 2.5 million barrels of oil per day in 2011 (Countries 2011, under "2011 World Oil Production").

In addition to importing commodities and oil, China embraces its relationship with Latin America as a way to access new markets to export its manufactured goods. China has had great success selling its products all over the world, often at a cheaper price than its competitors can provide.

Since a large portion of the Latin American population consists of working-class citizens, these cheaper products can be very appealing. This has led to a large increase in Chinese imports. For example, in Brazil, "Imports from China increased by twice the rate of those originating in other countries (39 percent versus 18 percent)" (Rosales 2012, under "Competition in Domestic Markets").

In addition to exporting its goods to Latin America, China is also interested in exporting its technologies. The Chinese government has voiced its intention to continue investing in infrastructure projects such as power plants, power grids and telecommunication facilities (Bruno 2012, para. 3). This allows companies like Huawei to continue its expansion in Latin America. Not only can Huawei sell its products, but it can build the infrastructure that supports its network.

China is not alone in the desire to pursue this relationship. Latin America also has a vested interest in

China.   Like China, the primary motivation for Latin America is trade.   "For the majority of governments in Latin America, the trade relationship with China has been a bonanza, producing much-needed trade surpluses" (Roett and Paz 2008, 17).   This economic boost has caused Latin America to pursue even more trade with China.   Trade between China and Latin America has increased about 30 percent annually since 2001 to reach $241.5 billion in 2011 (Li and Jianming 2012, para. 3).

The other main motivation for Latin America is foreign direct investment (FDI).   "One recent example are agreements between Brazil and China on satellite development, in which China provided 70 percent of the financing and technology and Brazil the remaining 30 percent" (Roett and Paz 2008, 18).   China has the ability to flood money into these countries seeking to benefit economically.

As evidence of this, "over 12% of combined Chinese outward FDI (financial and non-financial) had gone to the economies of Latin America and the Caribbean as of late 2009 (the region's stock was US$ 31 billion)" (Rosales and Kuwayama 2012, 33).

C.   CHALLENGES FACED

In its evolving relationship with China, Latin America has faced some challenges.   The flooding of the market with Chinese manufactured goods hinders industrial development in Mexico and Central American countries.   "Countries that rely on low-skilled, labor-intensive manufactured goods, in particular Mexico and Costa Rica, have suffered the worst effects" (Roett and Paz 2008, 17).   These Chinese goods are hindering growth in their domestic markets, as well as taking away the U.S. market from these countries.

An example of these challenges, Mexico filed a complaint to the World Trade Organization (WTO). In this complaint, Mexico cited, "significant price undercutting, price suppression, price depression, and lost sales in the United States" (China — Measures Relating to the Production and Exportation of Apparel and Textile Products 2012, under "Complaint by Mexico"). While some countries are benefiting from Chinese involvement in Latin America, it has clearly had some negative effects as well.

Francisco Gonzalez argues that the similarities in exports between China and Mexico are quite significant. The U.S. market export similarity index between China and Mexico rose continuously between the early 1970s and 2001, denoting more overlapped trade patterns and stronger competition (Gonzalez 2008, 149). While this could have negative impacts on China, it is actually more harmful to the Mexican economy because of its inability to compete with Chinese prices. Mexico relies on its trade with the U.S., and China's presence in this market hinders the growth of Mexico's economy.

This relationship also has negative implications for the South American countries. "The region will be vulnerable to the natural resource curse, in which foreign exchange earnings are obtained by the production of raw materials and commodities" (Roett and Paz 2008, 17). This is a curse because commodities will not last forever, and they are completely dependent on the market. "Latin America still faces the challenge of diversifying its

17

exports, moving beyond the raw commodities that China is so eager to buy, and further up the value-added scale" (Morris 2011, para. 3). While this is a challenge that must be addressed in the future, the trade between China and Latin America is still booming.

D. HUAWEI IN LATIN AMERICA

Huawei is a clear example of China's desire to pursue its relationships in Latin America, as the company's influence continues to grow in this region.

In recent years, Huawei has increased its expansion in Latin America exponentially. In fact, one of the most prominent forms of China's expansion is in the telecommunications industry. "Huawei now serves 50 operators in Latin America…and has built networks in 13 countries, including Argentina, Brazil, Chile, Colombia, Ecuador, Mexico, Uruguay and Venezuela" (How Huawei Advances 2008, 3).

This expansion has made Huawei one of the most powerful telecommunications companies in the region. Huawei claims to rank first in Internet Protocol Digital Subscriber Line Access Multiplexer (IP DSLAM) solution and Next Generation Networking (NGN) application in Latin America (Huawei Latin America Fact Sheet 2013, under "Latin America Operations"). As this field continues to grow, the profits from this investment will multiply as well.

It is clear that this expansion is not simply a short-term business venture. "As further proof of its long-term interest in the region, Huawei has established training centers in Brazil, Colombia, Mexico and Venezuela" (How

Huawei Advances 2008, 3). These training centers allow for the company to train its employees in Latin America, so they may operate at full potential in the region. This commitment to the future will allow Huawei to stay ahead of its competitors in the advancement of technology. This will ensure Huawei's status as the top telecommunications company in Latin America.

Brazil is one of the most significant regions in Latin America that Huawei has expanded. Huawei opened its Latin American distribution center, in Sorocaba, in the Brazilian state of Sao Paulo, where it has invested US$60 million (Chinese Group Huawei Opens Latin American Distribution Hub in Brazil 2012, para. 1). This investment has been seen through the deployment of 3G networks, the launching of Android phones, and the implementation of a Universal Mobile Telecommunications Systems (UMTS) (Huawei Latin America Fact Sheet 2013, under "Latin America Operations"). It is clear that Huawei is making great technological advances in Brazil. With Brazil being one of the fastest growing countries in the world, this is a natural place for investment from Huawei.

An example of success in Brazil is already apparent, as Huawei was one of the companies selected by a Brazilian vendor as one of its preferred 4G Long Term Evolution (LTE) equipment suppliers (TIM Brasil Picks NSN, Ericsson and Huawei to Deliver LTE 2012, para. 1). This shows a commitment to a long-term relationship between Huawei and Brazil. If Huawei continues to dominate competition in Latin America, it will continue to gain power and momentum in the region.

From the evidence shown, it is clear that Huawei is continuing to expand into the region's most powerful country of Brazil. However, Huawei is also expanding into the smaller, less developed countries, such as Trinidad & Tobago. Huawei was selected to upgrade the largest telecommunications company's mobile network and make it 4G compatible (Coalition: Cracks Growing 2012, 7).

Huawei introduced its fourth generation BTS (Base Transceiver Station) in this WiMAX network, which includes cutting-edge features like 4T4R (4 transmitters and 4 receivers) and MIMO (multi-input multi-output) (TSTT to Bridge Digital Divide in Trinidad and Tobago with Huawei's WiMAX Solution 2010, par 3). These advanced technologies are some of the reasons why Huawei is so popular in Latin America.

While it makes sense to invest in more developed regions because of the wealth available, it can also be beneficial to operate in a region with little competition. Trinidad & Tobago is a perfect example of this. Huawei can volunteer to build the infrastructure, as well as sell the mobile devices, which appeals to both the host country and telecommunications supplier.

Huawei also has significant ties with countries that the U.S. has had diplomatic disagreements with in the past. Venezuela's telecoms minister and the head of Telecom Venezuela met with Chinese counterparts and signed fresh partnership agreements with Huawei in 2007 (Anderson 2007, para. 5). This is not only an example of Huawei's continued expansion in the region, but also an example of Huawei's ties to U.S. adversaries.

While this may seem insignificant, there is a potential cause for concern. In 2011, Venezuelan diplomats were reportedly involved in planned cyberattacks against U.S. targets, including nuclear power plants (Smithson 2011, para. 1). Huawei could possess the technology needed to conduct these attacks successfully. Therefore, this is a relationship that should be monitored by concerned U.S. officials.

Another adversary that Huawei has had a relationship is Cuba. Huawei was consulted on projects such as the construction of an undersea cable between Venezuela and Cuba (Anderson 2007, para. 6). Until recently, there were too many restrictions for U.S. telecommunications companies to operate in Cuba. This was an opportunity for investment that Huawei was able to seize.

However, that may soon change. "Under the new policy, U.S. telecommunications providers will be able to establish fiber-optic cable and satellite telecommunications facilities linking the U.S. and Cuba" (Condon 2009, para. 3). This may provide some competition for Huawei in Cuba, but Huawei has the clear of advantage, having dealt with Cuba in the past.

Not only is Huawei expanding in countries that the U.S. considers adversaries, it is also expanding in Mexico, which the U.S. considers to be a close ally. Winning over customers helped Huawei's Mexico unit more than double sales to $440 million in 2010; from about $200 million in 2009 (Huawei's $30 Billion China Credit Opens Doors in Brazil, Mexico 2011, under "Market Gains").

While Mexico is America's closest ally in the region, it is also an immediate neighbor to the south. This shows the economic power that Huawei has just outside of U.S. borders. This is a significant amount of money that U.S. telecommunications companies are potentially losing out on because of Huawei's presence in Mexico.

Huawei has also recently launched Mexico's first LTE network. "Huawei's LTE services will cover nine Mexican cities, with plans to expand to 26 markets until the first quarter of 2013 to reach 65% of the country's population" (Rial 2012, para. 4). This is clear evidence of Huawei's expansion in Mexico. Since much of the country is rural, 65% is a significant amount of the country to provide LTE services. This will allow for Huawei's continued power in Mexico.

While it may seem as if Huawei is dominating technologies markets in Latin America, U.S. companies are not always willing to take the risk of a relationship in adversarial countries. Reportedly, "in May Costa Rica's government invited some of the world's biggest equipment manufacturers to build a sophisticated new mobile-telecoms network in the Central American country. Only Huawei stepped forward" (How Huawei Advances 2008, 3).

In cases like this, American companies had a chance to bid for the contract, but they declined. This shows that one of the reasons for Huawei's economic success in Latin America is the lack of U.S. investment in the region. If U.S. companies want to profit from Latin America, they need to be more aggressive in instances like this in Costa Rica.

In addition, Huawei's relationship with Costa Rica was soured over a difference in pricing. "Huawei had wanted to charge US$583m for the construction of 1.5m 3G lines—more than double the government's US$225m budget for the project" (How Huawei Advances 2008, 3). This damaged relationship left an opportunity for a U.S. company to step in and compete for the contract. Once again, this did not occur, leaving Huawei to negotiate a new deal.

While it appears that U.S. telecommunications companies may be disinterested in investing in Latin America, there is another possibility. These companies may fear that they cannot match Huawei's pricing, due to unfair practices. The European Union (EU) has accused Huawei of exactly this.

The EU has said that Huawei is inflicting damage on European producers by dumping products onto the European market at rock-bottom prices and selling equipment for wireless networks at least 35% below what it calls fair market prices (Dalton 2012, para. 3). U.S. companies can infer that it will be very similar in Latin America. This may be one reason that these companies hesitate to even attempt to compete with Huawei in the region.

There are multiple reasons why Huawei is so successful in expanding into areas like Latin America. One reason is the support it receives from the Chinese government. "Huawei continues to receive tax privileges and state-sponsored credit from Beijing, thanks to its designation as a 'national champion' of new technology" (How Huawei Advances 2008, 3). This relationship allows Huawei to spend more money in its pursuit of global expansion. This gives Huawei a great advantage over U.S. telecommunications companies, which are not sponsored by the government.

Another reason for Huawei's success in Latin America is the cheap labor it can provide. "China's vast, cheap labour force has allowed the company to offer products and services at a 20-30% discount to most of its competitors" (How Huawei Advances 2008, 3). This is an advantage that Chinese companies like Huawei have all over the world. However, it is even more relevant in Latin America, where much of the population lives in poverty.

This is an enormous advantage to have over U.S. companies, who can't compete with Huawei's prices. This is the case in most products, not simply telecommunications. It is a major hurdle faced by the U.S., and it still has no proven answer to the advantage cheap labor.

This economic advantage has specifically increased Huawei's expansion in Argentina. "In Argentina...when most foreign firms were retreating after the country's 2001/2 economic collapse, Huawei redoubled its efforts to penetrate the market" (How Huawei Advances 2008, 3). This shows not only Huawei's economic prowess, but its intelligence, as it invested in a target when all others backed out. This was another case in which U.S. companies had the opportunity to invest, but they opted not to, leaving the door open for Huawei.

One of the other major reasons for Huawei's success is technology. As mentioned earlier, Huawei is one of the leaders in mobile communications technology. However, Huawei is also ahead of its competition in providing this technology to the rural areas of Latin America. "With a market share of 67%, it remains the world's number-one producer of equipment using CDMA technology in the 450MHz band, which is popular in rural areas" (How Huawei Advances 2008, 3).

Rural telephony is an enormous advantage in a region like Latin America, where much of the region is made up of rural areas. Huawei was clearly looking to the future when they developed this technology. While other companies were focusing on the obvious need for communication in the large urban areas, Huawei took the less obvious route. This is clearly paying off already, and will likely continue to do so in the future, as other countries will be attempting to catch up.

It is clear that Huawei has made significant progress in its penetration of Latin America. It has done this through expanding into both economically powerful and poor countries. Examples of this were seen with Brazil and Trinidad and Tobago. Huawei has also struck deals with both U.S. adversaries, as well as allies. This was shown with the examples of Venezuela, Cuba, and Mexico. Finally, Huawei has expanded in countries that the U.S. opted not to pursue a relationship with. This was seen in both Costa Rica and Argentina.

There are multiple reasons why Huawei has been so successful in this region of the world. The first reason is its technology. As one of the world leaders in telecommunications, Huawei is clearly a top choice for some of these nations. Another reason that Huawei has been successful is the cheap labor it can provide. U.S. companies simply cannot match the prices that Huawei can offer. Finally, Huawei has penetrated countries because of the unwillingness of U.S. companies to invest. Whether this is because of the financial risk, or the political risk, the result is the same. Huawei is clearly gaining economic power in Latin America.

Now that it is clear that Huawei has gained economic power in Latin America, it is important to evaluate the strategic implications this has for the United States. The U.S. is clearly losing out on the potential telecommunications trade market in Latin America. While U.S. companies may wish this was not the case, it might be an obstacle that is very difficult to overcome.

As Huawei is the most powerful telecommunications company in Latin America, it has clearly dominated competition, particularly with U.S. companies in the region. As these countries in Latin America continue to work with the China-based Huawei, they may increase other forms of trade with China. This could limit the U.S. trade growth with these countries. As a nation's economic well-being is one of the key elements of security, this relationship does have negative implications for the United States. However, there are some ways in which the U.S. could mitigate this problem and limit the effects.

First, Huawei is the leading telecommunications infrastructure producer in the world. It will be difficult for any U.S. company to convince a country in Latin America that it can provide cheaper service than Huawei. If these companies want to compete in the region, they must first improve their technologies with research and development.

Second, U.S. companies will always struggle to compete with Chinese companies receiving government subsidies from Beijing. Huawei's cheap labor may be an insurmountable obstacle. The best option to deal with this issue is pursue legal options. If it can be proven that Huawei is using unfair trade practices, it may be forced to raise its prices by the WTO, creating a more fair market.

Finally, for U.S. companies to be more competitive in Latin America, they will have to take more risks and invest in these countries. Huawei will continue to win contracts in the region, as long as there are no other competitors. This includes countries that the U.S. has hesitated in dealing with in the past, such as Venezuela and Cuba.

E.   HUAWEI IN THE U.S.

In addition to expansion in Latin America, Huawei is also expanding in the United States. There are already a number of Huawei products available in the United States. Huawei entered the U.S. in 2007. Since then, it has been steadily building relationships with carriers, adding devices like smartphones, hot spots, and even a tablet (Dolcourt 2012, para. 6).

Best Buy, one of the most popular telecommunications technology providers in the U.S., currently carries four Huawei smartphones (Best Buy 2013, under "Mobile Phones"). While Huawei may not yet be a household name in the United States, it is definitely trending in that direction. With its advancements in technology and ability to provide cheap labor, Huawei will have clear advantages over U.S. companies if it continues to expand.

Huawei seems to be following the trend of other Chinese companies that continue to invest in the U.S. "Chinese direct investment in the United States is soaring…Businesses from China have established operations and created jobs in at least 35 of the 50 U.S. states" (Rosen and Hanemann 2011, 8).

Huawei's increase in products available in the U.S. shows that it too will follow this trend, and continue its expansion in the United States. This expansion has the potential to hurt U.S. companies economically, as they will likely be unable to compete with Huawei's prices.

The United States presents a logical option for Huawei's continued expansion. "After big successes in Africa, Latin America, and the Asia Pacific region, Huawei needs to find more room to expand. The U.S. holds obvious appeal" (Wohlsen 2012, para. 4). This appeal is due to the extensive amount of money spent on telecommunications each year. "The converging sectors of broadband, media and information technology add nearly $900 billion annually to the U.S. economy" (Broadband Industry Stats 2013, para. 2).

If Huawei does pursue expansion in the U.S., this should be alarming to other telecommunications companies, as they may struggle to compete. Huawei has the strength needed to have a huge impact on the market. "They bring a good financial position. They can create products. They've got a huge R&D capability. So they could be strong competitors" (Wohlsen 2012, para. 5). This ability to compete with U.S. companies makes Huawei's expansion even more probable.

Another country that has concerns about Huawei is Canada, who has taken a similar approach to the U.S. with Chinese investment in their country. The Canadian Security Intelligence Service (CSIS) recently warned against the Chinese bid for the energy company, Nexen. "They do not want to wake up one day and realize a crucial sector of the economy is under the control of foreign interests" (Ljunggren 2012, para. 3). This philosophy shows the growing global skepticism surrounding Chinese supported companies, like Huawei.

While this warning did not stop the Chinese bid for Nexen, it did make it much more difficult for them to acquire it. This could possibly deter both Chinese and Canadian companies from making similar deals with each other in the future. This is similar to the current strategy that the U.S. government has employed. Strict warnings against dealing with companies like Huawei have deterred some U.S. companies, but it might not continue to do so in the future.

Europe is another place where concerns over Huawei are growing. The European Commission has echoed similar statements to those made by U.S. officials about suspected Chinese government influence over Huawei. It believes "the Chinese government is subsidising it to allow Huawei to displace its competitors in European markets by artificially lowering the prices of its products" (Huawei Working with GCHQ to Quell Espionage Fears 2012, para. 3). This shows that the U.S. is not alone in its suspicion of Huawei. This global controversy is an example of another economic concern that Huawei presents.

THIS PAGE INTENTIONALLY LEFT BLANK

III. SECURITY CONCERNS SURROUNDING HUAWEI'S EXPANSION IN LATIN AMERICA

A.   INTRODUCTION

Although trade and common bonds are big reasons for U.S. interests in Latin America, another concern is security. "In the United States, we also know that we will not be safe at home unless our neighborhood is safe, so promoting security in the region is our first priority" (Reich 2002, under "Security"). In this case, promoting security could mean keeping out potentially harmful adversaries.

Chapter II showed that there are many economic reasons why Huawei could be considered a potential threat to the United States. It is now important to evaluate whether or not Huawei presents a security threat to the U.S. beyond the economic threat. In order to properly perform this evaluation, one must look at several factors.

The first factor is the many suspicions surrounding Huawei. Once all of the suspicions have been laid out, it is important to evaluate the evidence presented. Some suspicions are backed up by evidence, while in other cases, the evidence is lacking. One of the most important documents, which can show the evidence, or lack thereof, is the *Investigative Report on the U.S. National Security Issues Posed by Chinese Telecommunications Companies Huawei and ZTE* (Zhongxing Telecommunications Equipment Company Limited.

Once it is clear what solid evidence exists, it will be important to look at the circumstantial evidence, which is not ideal, but can provide support to some of the suspicions. Finally, it is crucial to examine what evidence is needed in order to provide proof for the claims made against Huawei.

B. SUSPICIONS REGARDING HUAWEI

1. Espionage

While Huawei has purportedly been very successful at illegally using its equipment and access to collect information, it has been surrounded by controversy. In recent years, the most glaring controversy in the U.S. is the suspicion of espionage. In February 2011, Huawei wrote a letter to the United States to address these concerns. "We sincerely hope that the United States government will carry out a formal investigation on any concerns it may have about Huawei" (Hu 2011, 5).

The U.S. accepted this invitation. The House Permanent Select Committee on Intelligence initiated this investigation in November 2011 to inquire into the counterintelligence and security threat posed by Chinese telecommunications companies doing business in the United States (Rogers and Ruppersberger 2012, iv).

One of the main focuses of the investigation was the suspicion of espionage. "Chinese actors are the world's most active and persistent perpetrators of economic espionage" (Foreign Spies Stealing US Economic Secrets in Cyberspace 2011, 5). These concerns about China led to similar suspicions of Huawei. The Committee spent a significant amount of time looking into these suspicions, and the connections between Huawei and the Chinese government made up a large part of the investigative report.

There are many ways in which a telecommunications company could conduct espionage. One way that this could be conducted is through the insertion of foreign devices into its telecommunications equipment. Malicious hardware or software could allow the Chinese government to shut down or degrade critical national security systems in a time of crisis (Rogers and Ruppersberger 2012, 3). This is one of the biggest reasons that officials do not want Huawei to expand into the Latin America or the U.S.

In addition to inserting hardware and software, Huawei could also use its personnel to conduct espionage. An example of this would be inserting a spy into Huawei's team of engineers. "To identify and resolve the issues, they will gain full access to network architecture and design - a security risk for network reconnaissance" (Ferro 2012, under "The security risk is the team of engineers"). This would be the case in any country in which Huawei installed the infrastructure.

If Huawei was to conduct such an operation, this would allow for easy reconnaissance. "As an attacker, knowing weak points, physical locations, logical layouts, what the target response plan is, and what equipment is all just marvellous intelligence" (Ferro 2012, under "What Security Actions are Possible"). All of these could potentially be gained by someone posing as an engineer or support technician. These are threats that should be concerning to nations hosting Huawei infrastructure in Latin America.

Not only is Latin America close to the United States geographically, but the U.S. maintains close relations with many of these countries. In addition, the U.S. military conducts operations in Latin America. The U.S. operates over twenty military bases throughout Latin America (Whitney Jr. 2012, para. 1). An attack on the infrastructure there could have serious impact on military communications.

2. Intellectual Property Infringement

In addition to Huawei's possible connections with the government, they have also been accused of intellectual property infringement. In February 2003 Cisco Systems, sued Huawei Technologies for allegedly infringing on its patents and illegally copying source code used in its routers and switches (Baxter 2003, under "Cisco's Motion for Preliminary Injunction"). This accusation shows a lack of trust in Huawei from U.S. companies.

More recently, in January 2013, the United States International Trade Commission launched a new patent probe against Huawei. This probe will investigate InterDigital's complaints of patent violation on its 3G and 4G devices (Certain Wireless Devices with 3G and/or 4G Capabilities and Components Thereof 2013, para. 1). This shows that there are similar suspicions surround Huawei in the U.S. ten years after the accusations were launched by Cisco. This pattern of potentially illegal activity is one of the reasons the U.S. is very cautious when dealing with Huawei.

3. Relationship with Iran

In addition to potential cyber espionage and intellectual property infringement, the U.S. is suspicious of Huawei's relationship with Iran. Iran has been labeled a threat by the United States due to its rogue government and pursuit of nuclear weapons. Huawei is suspected in assisting the Iranian government with several technological projects. One example is a project in which Huawei was suspected of assisting the Iranian police in tracking people's cell phones.

This is not the only concerning link between Huawei and Iran. Huawei is also suspected of selling American antenna equipment to Iran. This is contrary to prior statements from Huawei, stating that it would abide by U.S. embargoes set against Iran. If true, these suspicions would clearly show a violation of these embargoes.

Huawei is not the only Chinese company suspected of selling U.S. equipment to Iran. China's ZTE Corp is suspected of selling U.S. computer gear to an Iranian telecommunications firm. While Huawei is the focus of this case study, confirming these suspicions would show that Iran is clearly using these Chinese telecommunications companies to acquire U.S. equipment, which could potentially be used against the U.S. in a future conflict.

One of the companies voicing these suspicions is Hewlett-Packard (HP). They addressed the suspicion of these embargoes. "HP's distribution contract terms prohibit the sale of HP products into Iran and require compliance with U.S. and other applicable export laws" (Stecklow, "Huawei Partner Offered Embargoed HP Gear to Iran" 2012, para. 7).

If Huawei is not abiding by the same regulations as American companies, it should be taken into account when evaluating the threat that Huawei presents.

4. Other Global Suspicions

In addition to the allegations the U.S. has brought against Huawei, the telecommunications company has faced controversies all over the world. One such controversy was in Algeria, where two Huawei officers were accused of bribery and corruption. This would show not only the illegal activity conducted by representatives of Huawei in Africa, but the potential to perform similar actions in Latin America.

In addition, the European Commission shares similar security concerns as the U.S. "They have also voiced concerns that in case of open war, the Chinese government might use its influence over Huawei to disable the company's equipment built into infrastructure across the world" (Huawei Working with GCHQ to Quell Espionage Fears 2012, para. 3).

This could leave China's adversaries vulnerable and without communication capabilities. This possibility is concerning for both the U.S. and countries in Europe that foresee any type of conflict with China in the future.

Finally, Huawei has recently been linked to the death of an American engineer in Singapore. "Shane Todd, the engineer, headed a team at the Institute of Microelectronics (IME) that worked on the development of gallium nitride, a substance that can be used in both commercial and military applications" (Spolar and Bonner

2013, para. 2). The suspicions surrounding this case imply that Huawei was interested in gallium nitride for military purposes. This association with the death, as well as the research of gallium nitride should be concerning to U.S. officials.

C.   EVIDENCE OF ESPIONAGE

1.   Evidence Presented

After an extensive review of current documents, it is clear that there is no solid evidence supporting claims of Huawei's espionage. While there may be strong suspicions, lack of evidence to the contrary, and circumstantial evidence, there is currently no proof that Huawei is performing espionage. This is certainly not due to a lack of effort to find such evidence. Either Huawei is not conducting such acts, or it is very successful at covering up its activities.

2.   Evidence Missing

In order to properly prove the suspicions of espionage, someone must provide some form of evidence against Huawei. Since none has been found to date, any type of proof would lend some validity to the accusations. This evidence could come in many different forms.

One type of evidence that is missing is physical evidence. If some type of espionage tool was discovered in a piece of Huawei hardware or software, this would certainly validate these suspicions. However, nobody has found anything of the sort in past investigations.

A second type of evidence that is missing is documentation. There are no documents that have been found linking Huawei to espionage. An example of a valuable document would be one linking Huawei to the People's Liberation Army (PLA), showing that it was performing espionage missions that were assisting the PLA.

A third potential type of evidence would be a statement from an insider. No current or former employees of Huawei have admitted to conducting espionage for the company. A statement from a Huawei or Chinese government employee that linked Huawei to espionage could potentially be the lead needed to find solid evidence.

Until one of these types of evidence is discovered, it will be difficult to validate claims of Huawei conducting espionage. Without this proof, it may be hard to limit Huawei's continued global expansion.

D. EVIDENCE OF INTELLECTUAL PROPERTY INFRINGEMENT

1. Evidence Presented

In the 2003 case of Cisco's claim against Huawei for patent infringement, there is significantly more evidence supporting the claim. "Huawei admitted that some of the code used in its products came from an outside and unauthorized source" (Reardon 2003, para. 2). This admission forced Huawei to change all of its products in order to comply, leaving its claim to innocence on the subject unbelievable. This is an example of much stronger evidence presented against Huawei.

In the 2013 United States International Trade Commission probe, the outcome is still pending.

Unfortunately, there is very little evidence related to this case available to the public at this time.

2. Evidence Missing

From the evidence presented, it is clear that Huawei was guilty of intellectual property infringement against Cisco, in 2003. No further evidence is needed, since Huawei admitted guilt and was forced to change its products to comply with the court. However, this is a case from ten years ago, and it does not prove that Huawei is still conducting patent infringement against other companies.

In order to prove that Huawei is still guilty of this type of activity, the current case, launched by the International Trade Commission, needs to provide similar evidence. If this evidence does exist, it will present a clear threat to U.S. companies.

E. EVIDENCE OF AN INAPPROPRIATE RELATIONSHIP WITH IRAN

1. Evidence Presented

Huawei is suspected of making multiple deals with Iranian companies and government agencies. The first suspicion was installing the tracking capability. According to sources, "Huawei recently signed a contract to install equipment for a system at Iran's largest mobile-phone operator that allows police to track people based on the locations of their cellphones" (Stecklow, Fassihi and Chao 2011, 3).

This shows not only a partnership with a U.S. adversary, but also the capability to track its customers' cellphones. While this is not an uncommon telecommunications capability, sharing this technology with Iran could potentially be a security concern, as tensions between the U.S. and Iran remain high.

In addition to being able to track the location of the phones, Huawei also provided another significant capability, "supporting the special requirements from security agencies to monitor in real time the communication traffic between subscribers" (Stecklow, How Foreign Firms Tried to Sell Spy Gear to Iran 2012, para. 7). This capability is much more concerning, giving some credence to the suspicion of Chinese espionage. While this is not evidence of Huawei spying on customers, it shows that they not only have the capability, but they are willing to share that capability with Iran.

The second suspicion was that of Huawei selling U.S. antenna equipment to Iran. Documents obtained by international news agency Reuters show that an Iranian partner of Huawei Technologies, a company that has denied breaking U.S. sanctions, tried to sell embargoed American antenna equipment to an Iranian firm (Stecklow, Huawei Partner Offered U.S. Tech to Iran 2012, para. 1). This shows a very suspicious relationship between Huawei and Iran.

This willingness to violate U.S. sanctions with Iran presents a potential security threat. Huawei could avoid other U.S. laws in the future or even assist Iran in future operations against the United States.

In addition to Huawei, ZTE was also suspected of providing U.S. equipment to Iran. According to sources, China's ZTE Corp had sold or agreed to sell millions of dollars worth of U.S. computer gear to Telecommunication Co. of Iran, the country's largest telecommunications firm (Stecklow, Huawei Partner Offered U.S. Tech to Iran 2012, para. 10).

While these contracts and documents have not been made publicly available, the sources are considered reliable. This is a significant amount of evidence linking Huawei with Iran. It also shows Huawei's unwillingness to abide by U.S. embargoes set against Iran, which it claimed it would follow. This evidence shows a possible security risk.

2.   Evidence Missing

While it has been stated that these contracts and documents exist, it would be more convincing to the public if they were readily available for anyone to read. This is a simple solution that would lead to a stronger case against Huawei.

In addition to providing the documentation to support claims against Huawei's relationship with Iran, it would also help to provide evidence of intent. While it is clear that Huawei has made deals with Iran, there is no proof that either side has malicious intent against the United States. If one could prove that the sale of the cellphone tracking technology, U.S. antenna equipment, or U.S. computer gear were intended to cause harm to the U.S., this would be sufficient evidence of Huawei's security threat.

F.   EVIDENCE OF OTHER GLOBAL CONTROVERSIES

1.   Evidence Presented

In the case of Algeria, the two Huawei officers were sentenced to 10 years in prison for bribery and corruption in Algeria, but have since been whisked away from Algeria to China, and Huawei has refused to return them to face the law (Dowuona 2012, para. 14). This shows not only the illegal activity conducted by representatives of Huawei, but also Huawei's powerful connection with the Chinese government.

One of the reasons this particular case is concerning is the many parallels between China's penetration into Africa and their expansion in Latin America. Both Africa and Latin America are made up of many regions with a lot of poverty. Huawei saw these regions as a potential for expansion, offering to build the infrastructure at a low cost for their telecommunications networks. This parallel shows that these problems in Algeria could very easily happen in Latin America as well.

In the case of the death of Shane Todd, there is some evidence linking Todd to Huawei. High quality global journalism requires investment. "Mr Todd's parents said they found among his possessions an external hard drive that contained work files—including one, labelled "Huawei", that appears to be a plan between IME and Huawei for the development of gallium nitride" (Spolar and Bonner 2013, para. 3). This evidence supports the claim that Huawei was working with Todd on this matter.

In addition to the suspicion of developing gallium nitride for military purposes, Huawei is also suspected in the death of Shane Todd. "Mr Todd's parents, Rick and Mary Todd of Montana, have said that their son told them frequently in 2012 that he was worried that he was compromising US national security with his work on a project at IME that involved a Chinese company" (Spolar and Bonner 2013, para. 11). These statements from the family make Huawei a viable suspect in the case of Todd's death.

2. Evidence Missing

While the case in Algeria clearly shows illegal activity conducted by Huawei, the European Commission has not presented any proof of Huawei's plans to disable infrastructure in foreign countries. Like the U.S. Committee, GCHQ has not provided evidence that Huawei has these plans in mind. However, if this were the case, it could leave China's adversaries vulnerable and without communication capabilities. Even though there is little evidence, the mere possibility is concerning for both the U.S. and countries in Europe that foresee any type of conflict with China in the future.

In order to justify further legal action against Huawei, there needs to be more evidence presented. One form of evidence would be to show a pattern of illegal activity, like in Algeria. If this was shown to be a common theme, rather than a single occurrence, it would give more leverage to the argument against Huawei's expansion.

Another form of evidence would be proof of the European Commission's fears of Huawei disabling its equipment built into infrastructure around the world during a war. First, there would need to be proof that this task is possible. Once that is determined, the amount of influence that the Chinese government has over Huawei would need to be evaluated. Finally, proof of this intent would need to be presented. Not only have they not all been presented, but none of these forms of evidence have been presented by GCHQ.

The last global controversy was the death of Shane Todd. While the discovered hard drive linked Huawei to Todd and gallium nitride, there is little evidence proving what intent there was in this development. In order to prove that this was for military purposes, some documentation of this intent must be provided.

In the case of Todd's death, it is clear that his family suspects Huawei of foul play. However, this is the only proof available at this time. In order to prove wrongdoing, it will be important that the Singapore police investigate the matter further, providing a motive and physical evidence to support the family's claims.

G. HPSCI INVESTIGATION

In November 2011, the House Permanent Select Committee on Intelligence launched an investigation to accommodate Huawei's request. While Huawei requested this investigation, the Committee found the company less than cooperative. "Huawei, in particular, failed to provide thorough information about its corporate structure, history, ownership, operations, financial arrangements, or management" (Rogers and Ruppersberger 2012, v). This ambiguity raised further concerns regarding Huawei during the investigation.

This investigation did not provide an overwhelming amount of evidence against Huawei, with no evidence of cyber espionage. However, during the investigation, Huawei was not fully cooperative with the Committee. They claimed to have no knowledge of Chinese laws that force them to comply with the Chinese government's requests for access to their equipment (Rogers and Ruppersberger 2012, 10). The Committee found this claim to be unbelievable. According to Rogers and Ruppersberger, Huawei was also very vague and incomplete in answering most questions that were presented. This lack of cooperation only added to the Committee's suspicions of the company.

While no evidence of Huawei conducting espionage was discovered, the Committee attempted to draw a link between Huawei and the Chinese government, the Communist party, and the People's Liberation Army (PLA). The Committee did find documentation of "Huawei employees showing that Huawei provides special network services to an entity the employee believes to be an elite cyber-warfare unit within the PLA" (Rogers and Ruppersberger 2012, 34). The report cites an internal Huawei email, but does not provide the actual email. This is the closest that the Committee came to providing evidence of Huawei conducting cyber espionage.

While the link between Huawei and the PLA was limited in terms of evidence, the Committee was successful in discovering another area of concern. "The Intelligence Committee's investigation into the security of Huawei's router software reportedly found it 'riddled with holes,' many of which could potentially be exploited by hackers" (McAllister 2012, under "Bugs, Just Not the Spying Kind").

While this was not the main focus of the investigation, it was an important finding.

It is unknown whether these software vulnerabilities are intentional or accidental. If they are intentional, Huawei could be leaving backdoors in the software in order to access the routers in the future. This would be a clear reason to distrust Huawei and its equipment. If the vulnerabilities are accidental, it is simply sloppy coding, which is also a risk that the U.S. should not be willing to take with its computer equipment. Either way, it is clear that further investigation needs to be done on the subject in order to produce more evidence.

While many would assume that Huawei would deny these vulnerabilities, this was not the case. "A move to engage one of its biggest critics is a significant shift in Huawei's approach to dealing with the issue, indicating the security concerns may not be entirely baseless" (Alo 2012). If there was no legitimacy to these security concerns, Huawei would continue to ignore the criticism it receives. This shows that Huawei's routers are indeed vulnerable, but there is still no evidence to support malicious intent.

IV. CONCLUSION AND RECOMMENDATIONS

A. CONCLUSION

From the previous examples, it is clear that Huawei is a company that is surrounded by much controversy, and its penetration into Latin America should be viewed with much caution. These controversies include both economic and security concerns. There are many claims and accusations presented against Huawei, and each of these suspicions is supported by varying amounts of evidence.

The first argument that was presented was that Huawei's penetration into Latin America presents an economic threat to the United States. The evidence presented shows that Huawei is already the leading telecommunications company in Latin America. The evidence also shows that U.S. companies are losing out on potential business in the region, whether by being under bid by Huawei or choosing to not work on specific contracts.

There are two major reasons for this. The first is that U.S. companies are not taking the same risk with investment in Latin America. The only solution for this problem is for American companies to take more risks in the region. The second reason is the ability of Huawei to use cheap labor to keep its prices low. The only way for the U.S. to counter this is to prove unfair trade practices, forcing Huawei to raise its prices.

The second strategic implication of Huawei's penetration into Latin America is the security concern. The arguments presented show that there are many accusations that have been launched against Huawei. However, there is not always evidence provided to support such allegations.

The first suspicion of Huawei that was presented was that of espionage. While this is a very serious allegation, with tremendous repercussions for the United States, very little evidence exists thus far to support validate these suspicions. Therefore, at this time, it is hard to consider Huawei a viable threat to national security. At the same time, little evidence presently exists to absolve Huawei either. Vigilant observation is merited.

The second suspicion was that of stealing intellectual property. This is a threat that was not only supported by evidence, but there was a pattern presented, as Huawei as now been accused of similar activity just this year. This is a viable threat to the economic security of U.S. or Latin American companies, whose patents may be at risk. In addition, it shows the willingness of Huawei to conduct illegal activities, implying a possible willingness to partake in other illegal actions.

The third accusation dealt with Huawei's relationship with Iran. Evidence was presented showing a clear relationship between Huawei and Iran, but the extent of this relationship is still unclear. It is clear that Huawei has violated U.S. embargoes against Iran, but it is not clear if there is malicious intent, or if this is simply an economic move. However, the trade of technology shows the capability, now shared by Huawei and Iran, presents a threat on its own.

Finally, while these threats were being investigated, it was also revealed that Huawei products contained code vulnerabilities, leading to a lack of security (McAllister 2012, under "Bugs, just not the spying kind"). This is an equally concerning threat, as it leaves customers, whether from the U.S. or Latin America, at risk to cyber-attacks. There was no evidence provided suggesting that these were intentional holes left in the equipment, but the threat is no less significant to the users.

B.   RECOMMENDATIONS

While there was some evidence to support accusations launched against Huawei, many claims still require supporting evidence. Therefore, if the U.S. wishes to continue these accusations, pursuit of this evidence is necessary. Otherwise, U.S. officials will not be able to advocate for limiting Huawei's expansion into Latin America.

First, U.S. officials need to produce evidence of espionage. This can be done through Huawei's hardware and software, or through documents linking it to conducting espionage for the PLA or Chinese government. If this type of evidence cannot be found, it is recommended that these claims no longer be made, as it is difficult to support, and the lack of evidence could cause the public to be skeptical of any Huawei wrongdoing.

Second, further proof of stealing intellectual property would support claims against allowing Huawei's continued expansion. If the current case pending against Huawei proves that it is still violating patents, this will be enough evidence to support these claims.

49

Third, further investigation into Huawei's relationship with Iran is required to prove a possible security threat. It is recommended that U.S. officials look for proof of Huawei's malicious intent, showing it knowingly sold U.S. equipment to Iran to harm the United States. This evidence will convince authorities that Huawei is not a company that should be trusted by U.S. companies.

If the previous examples of evidence are found, it will be clear that Huawei's expansion is a threat to U.S. security. If this evidence is not produced, it will be hard for the U.S. to convince civilian companies not to work with Huawei. However, it should not be difficult to keep government agencies from using Huawei products. Even without further evidence, the current findings show that Huawei should not be trusted to be used for government purposes.

C. BENEFITS OF RESEARCH TO THE DEPARTMENT OF DEFENSE (DOD)

This research benefits the DOD by raising questions regarding the penetration of Huawei into the Latin American telecommunications infrastructure. The research presented shows the necessity for further investigation into Huawei. There may be limited evidence; however, the serious accusations discussed earlier indicate a potential security threat to the U.S. presented by Huawei.

The most concerning accusation against Huawei is that the company has built the ability for Huawei, rather than the nation owning the infrastructure, to shut down the infrastructure during a time of war. This should be of great concern in the case of Latin America, where the United States conducts many military operations. As Huawei's penetration into Latin America increases, military communications could be forced to travel on a Huawei-based infrastructure. If this infrastructure could be shut down through an intentional backdoor, it could leave U.S. military operations extremely vulnerable.

In addition, Huawei's relationship with Iran should concern the DOD. If Huawei is selling American equipment to Iran with malicious intent, this is clearly a threat to U.S. security. This matter should be investigated further and appropriate actions taken.

These accusations show why the DOD should be concerned about Huawei's continued expansion. If there is truth to the accusations, Huawei's presence in Latin America is a threat to U.S. security because of America's close relationship and military presence in the region. These concerns will be further amplified for the DOD if Huawei continues its expansion in the United States. This is why there is a need for further investigation into Huawei.

THIS PAGE INTENTIONALLY LEFT BLANK

LIST OF REFERENCES

Albanesius, Chloe. 2013. "Apple, Samsung Take Smartphone
    Lead Ahead of Huawei." *PC Magazine,* February, 13.
    Accessed February 16, 2013.
    http://www.pcmag.com/article2/0,2817,2415400,00.asp.

Alo, Bob Prince. 2012. "Huawei to Work With German Hacker."
    Midsize Insider. November 7. Accessed January 21,
    2013. http://midsizeinsider.com/en-us/article/huawei-
    to-work-with-german-hacker.

Baxter, Sam F. 2013. "Cisco's Motion for Preliminary
    Injunction." *Cisco.* February 5. Accessed January 21,
    2013.
    http://newsroom.cisco.com/dlls/Cisco_Mot_for_PI.pdf.

Best Buy. 2013. Huawei Products Search. Accessed February
    9, 2013.
    http://www.bestbuy.com/site/searchpage.jsp?_dyncharset
    =ISO-8859-
    1&_dynSessConf=&id=pcat17071&type=page&sc=Global&cp=1&
    nrp=15&sp=&qp=&list=n&iht=y&usc=All+Categories&ks=960&
    st=huawei.

Bruno, Roberta. 2012. "Chinese Interest in Latin America's
    Growth." *Council on Hemishperic Affairs.* July 25.
    Accessed January 27, 2013.
    http://www.coha.org/chinese-interest-in-latin-
    americas-growth/.

"Chinese Group Huawei Opens Latin American Distribution Hub
    in Brazil." *Macau Hub.* June 1, 2012. Accessed January
    21, 2013.
    http://www.macauhub.com.mo/en/2012/06/01/chinese-
    group-huawei-opens-latin-american-distribution-hub-in-
    brazil/.

"Cloud+." *Huawei Device.* n.d. Accessed January 21, 2013.
    http://www.huaweidevice.co.in/cloud/.

"Coalition: Cracks Growing." 2012 *Latin America Monitor:
    Caribbean Monitor,* 29: 7.

Condon, Stephanie. 2009. "Obama Eases U.S.-Cuba Telecom
    Restrictions." *CNET.* April 13. Accessed February 9,

2013. http://news.cnet.com/8301-13578_3-10218521-
38.html

Crandall, Russell, and Britta Crandall. 2008. "Brazil: Ally
or Rival?". In The United States and Latin America
after the Cold War, 145-161. New York: Cambridge
University Press

Crandall, Russell, and Katie Hunter. 2008. "The United
States and Mexico." In *The United States and Latin
America after the Cold War*, by Russell Crandall, 213-
243. New York: Cambridge University Press.

Dalton, Matthew. 2012. "EU Weighs Steps Over Huawei, ZTE
Pricing." *Wall Street Journal.* December 7. Accessed
February 9, 2013.
http://online.wsj.com/article/SB1000142412788732331680
4578165231686297180.html.

Dillet, Romain. 2013. "Huawei Released 85% of Its Devices
Under Its Own Brand in 2012 Compared to 20% in 2011."
Tech Crunch. January 2. Accessed January 21, 2013.
http://techcrunch.com/2013/01/02/huawei-released-85-
percent-of-its-devices-under-its-own-brand-in-2012-
compared-to-20-percent-in-2011/.

"Discovering Huawei's History." *Into China*. August 7, 2012.
Accessed January 21, 2013.
http://intochina.asia/discovering-huaweis-history/.

Dolcourt, Jessica. 2012. "Huawei Desperate to Crack the
Top-Tier U.S. Brands." *CNET*. October 10. Accessed
January 21, 2013. http://reviews.cnet.com/8301-
12261_7-57530039-10356022/huawei-desperate-to-crack-
the-top-tier-u.s-brands/.

EIU Country Analysis. 2008. *Latin America/China telecoms:
How Huawei Advances* Sep 15. New York, NY: Alacra Store

Dowuona, Samuel Nii Narku. 2012. "Huawei Implicated in
Illegal Involvement in Ghana's Politics." *My Joy
Online*. October 17. Accessed January 21, 2013.
http://business.myjoyonline.com/pages/news/201210/9567
7.php.

Ferro, Greg. 2012. "The Huawei Security Problem Isn't the
Hardware, It's Engineers Fixing the Bugs." *Ethereal*

Mind. October 29. Accessed February 17, 2013.
http://etherealmind.com/the-huawei-security-problem-
isnt-the-hardware-its-engineers-fixing-the-bugs/.

Office of the National Counterintelligence Executive.2011.
*Foreign Spies Stealing US Economic Secrets in
Cyberspace, report to Congress on Foreign Economic
Collection and Industrial Espionage,* Washington DC:
Office of the National Counterintelligence Executive.

Gonzalez, Francisco E. n.d. "Latin America in the Economic
Equation-Winners and Losers: What Can Losers Do?" In
China's Expansion into the Western Hemisphere. Edited
by Riordan Roett and Guadalupe Paz, 148-165.
Washington, D.C.: Brookings Institution Press.

Grudgings, Stuart, and Simon Gardner. 2011. "Rising China
Threatens U.S. Clout in Latin America." *Reuters.* March
16. Accessed January 24, 2013.
http://www.reuters.com/article/2011/03/16/us-
latinamerica-china-idUSTRE72F19C20110316.

Hu, Ken. 2011. "Huawei Open Letter." *Wall Street Journal.*
February 5. Accessed February 3, 2013.
http://online.wsj.com/public/resources/documents/Huawe
i20110205.pdf.

"Huawei Cloud Congress 2012 Shows How Enterprises Can 'Make
IT Simple, Make Business Agile' in the Cloud Era."
Huawei. September 5, 2012. Accessed January 21, 2013.
http://www.huawei.com/en/about-huawei/newsroom/press-
release/latest/hw-187499-hcc2012.htm.

"Huawei Latin America Fact Sheet." *Huawei.* 2013. Accessed
February 9, 2013. http://www.huawei.com/us/about-
huawei/newsroom/resources/latin_america/index.htm.

"Huawei Partner Offered Embargoed HP Gear to Iran."
Reuters. December 30, 2012. Accessed February 5, 2103.
http://www.reuters.com/article/2012/12/30/us-iran-
huawei-hp-idUSBRE8BT0BF20121230.

"Huawei Partner Offered U.S. Tech to Iran." *Reuters.*
October 25, 2012. Accessed February 5, 2013.
http://www.reuters.com/article/2012/10/25/us-huawei-
iran-idUSBRE89O0E520121025.

"Huawei Working with GCHQ to Quell Espionage Fears." *The H.*
August 7, 2012. Accessed January 21, 2013.
http://www.h-online.com/security/news/item/Report-
Huawei-working-with-GCHQ-to-quell-espionage-fears-
1661205.html.

"Huawei's $30 Billion China Credit Opens Doors in Brazil,
Mexico." *Bloomber.* April 24, 2011. Accessed January
21, 2013. http://www.bloomberg.com/news/2011-04-
25/huawei-counts-on-30-billion-china-credit-to-open-
doors-in-brazil-mexico.html.

Iseman, Maria. 2012. "Top Ten Countries with which the U.S.
Trades." *United States Census Bureau.* Accessed
February 16, 2013. http://www.census.gov/foreign-
trade/top/dst/current/balance.html.

Kusnetzky, Dan. 2010. "What is "Big Data?"." *ZD Net.*
February 16. Accessed February 16, 2013.
http://www.zdnet.com/blog/virtualization/what-is-big-
data/1708.

"Lat-Ams Left-wing Govts Advance on Plan for Joint Telecoms
Firm." *Cellular-News.* November 8, 2007. Accessed
January 21, 2013. http://www.cellular-
news.com/story/27262.php.

Li, Jiabao, and Zhang Jianming. 2012. "Deeper Sino-Latin
American Trade Cooperation Urged." *China Daily.*
October 18. Accessed February 9, 2013.
http://www.chinadaily.com.cn/cndy/2012-
10/18/content_15826118.htm.

Ljunggren, David. 2012. "Insight: Security Fears Dogged
Canada Debate on China Energy Bid." *Reuters.* December
23. Accessed January 21, 2013.
http://www.reuters.com/article/2012/12/23/us-
investment-security-idUSBRE8BM0C620121223.

McAllister, Neil. 2012. "Huawei, ZTE Probe Showed No
Evidence of Spying." *Register.* October 18. Accessed
January 21, 2013.
http://www.theregister.co.uk/2012/10/18/huawei_spying_
probe_returned_nothing/print.html.

Moronde, Jose A. 2003. "Chile: The Invisible Hand and
Contemporary Foreign Policy." In Latin American and

Caribbean Foreign Policy. Edited by Frank O. Mora and
    Jeanne A.K. Hey, 243-263. Boulder, Colorado: Rowman
    and Littlefield.

Morris, Ruth. 2011. "China: Latin America Trade Jumps."
    Latin Business Chronicle. May 9. Accesssed January 24,
    2013.
    http://www.latinbusinesschronicle.com/app/article.aspx
    ?id=4893.

Morrison, Julian, and Ewa Romaniuk. n.d. "KPNI Builds
    Cloud-based "One IT Factory" to Reduct Costs." *Huawei*.
    Accessed January 21, 2013.
    http://www.huawei.com/ilink/en/solutions/arpu-
    up/morematerial-a/HW_116200.

Muncaster, Phil. 2012. "New Quad-Core Mobile Chip Will Mean
    Cheaper High-End Smartphones." *Technology Review*.
    December 12. Accessed January 21, 2013.
    http://www.technologyreview.com/news/508696/new-quad-
    core-mobile-chip-will-mean-cheaper-high-end-
    smartphones/.

"Noah's Ark Lab." *Noah's Ark Lab*. n.d. Accessed January 21,
    2013. http://www.noahlab.com.hk/.

Reardon, Marguerite. 2013. "Huawei Admits Copying." *Light
    Reading*. March 25. Accessed February 4, 2013.
    http://www.lightreading.com/ip-convergence/huawei-
    admits-copying/240020439.

Reich, Otto. 2002. "U.S. Interests in Latin America." *The
    Heritage Foundation*. October 31. Accessed January 26,
    2013.
    http://www.heritage.org/research/reports/2002/10/us-
    interests-in-latin-america.

"Ren Zhengfei." 2012. *Forbes*. March. Accessed February 16,
    2013. http://www.forbes.com/profile/zhengfei-ren/.

Rial, Nerea. 2012. "Telcel, Huawei Launch Commercial LTE
    Network in Mexico." *NewEurope*. November 21. Accessed
    January 21, 2013.
    http://www.neurope.eu/article/telcel-huawei-launch-
    commercial-lte-network-mexico.

Roett, Riordan, and Guadalupe Paz. n.d. "Introduction." In
    China's Expansion into the Western Hemisphere. Edited
    by Riordan Roett and Guadalupe Paz, 1-20. Washington,
    D.C.: Brookings Institution Press

Rosales, Osvaldo. 2012. "Trade Competition from China."
    Quarterly Americas. Winter. Accessed February 9, 2013.
    http://americasquarterly.org/Rosales.

Rosales, Osvaldo, and Mikio Kuwayama. 2012. *China and Latin
    America: Building a Strategic Economic and Trade
    Relationship*. Santiago: Economic Commission for Latin
    America and the Caribbean.

Rosen, Daniel H, and Thilo Hanemann. 2011. An American Open
    Door? Maximizing the Benefits of Chinese Foreign
    Direct Investment. Special Report. New York: Asia
    Society.

Shao, Ken. 2012. "History is the key to understanding
    Huawei." *The Conversation*. April 3. Accessed January
    21, 2013. http://theconversation.edu.au/history-is-
    the-key-to-understanding-huawei-5994.

Smithson, S. 2011. "U.S. Authorities Probing Alleged
    Cyberattack Plot by Venezuela, Iran." *Washington
    Times*. December 13. Accessed February 9, 2013.
    http://www.washingtontimes.com/news/2011/dec/13/us-
    probing-alleged-cyberattack-plot-iran-
    venezuela/?page=all.

Spolar, Christine, and Raymond Bonner. 2013. "Huawei Says
    Singapore Agency Project Was Not Pursued." *The
    Financial Times*. February 22. Accessed February 24,
    2013. http://www.ft.com/intl/cms/s/0/dfe8e21a-7cf7-
    11e2-adb6-00144feabdc0.html#axzz2LqYk32uK.

Stecklow, Steve. 2012. "How Foreign Firms Tried to Sell Spy
    Gear to Iran." *Reuters*. December 5. Accessed February
    17, 2013.
    http://www.reuters.com/article/2012/12/05/us-huawei-
    iran-idUSBRE8B409820121205.

Stecklow, Steve, Farnaz Fassihi, and Loretta Chao. 2011.
    "Chinese Tech Giant Aids Iran." *The Wall Street
    Journal*. October 27. Accessed January 21, 2013.

http://online.wsj.com/article/SB1000142405297020464450
4576651503577823210.html.

The New Challenge: China in the Western Hemisphere: *Hearing Before the Subcommittee on the Western Hemisphere of the Committee on Foreign Affairs*110th Cong.(2008) (statement of Eliot L. Engel, congressional representative from New York). 1-37.

"TIM Brasil Picks NSN, Ericsson and Huawei to Deliver LTE." *TeleGeography*. October 31, 2012. Accessed January 21, 2013. http://www.telegeography.com/products/commsupdate/arti cles/2012/10/31/tim-brasil-picks-nsn-ericsson-and-huawei-to-deliver-lte/.

"TSTT to Bridge Digital Divide in Trinidad and Tobago with Huawei's WiMAX Solution." *Huawei*. December 7, 2010. Accessed February 9, 2013. http://www.huawei.com/en/about-huawei/newsroom/press-release/hw-062599-tstt-wimax.htm.

U.S. Energy Information Administration. 2011."Countries." Accessed February 9, 2013. http://www.eia.gov/countries/index.cfm?view=production.

U.S. House of Representatives. House Permanent Select Committee on Intelligence. *Investigative Report on the U.S. National Security Issues Posed by Chinese Telecommunications Companies Huawei and ZTE.* Washington: Government Printing Office, 2012.

U.S. International Trade Commission, "USITC Institutes Section 337 Investigation of Certain Wireless Devices with 3G and/or 4G Capabilities and Components Thereof," news release, January 30, 2013, http://www.usitc.gov/press_room/news_release/2013/er01 30l11.htm

US Telecom, the Broadband Association. "Broadband Industry Stats." 2013. Accessed February 9, 2013. http://www.ustelecom.org/broadband-industry/broadband-industry-stats.

Whitney Jr., W.T. 2012. "United States Adds Bases in South America." *People's World*. April 26. Accessed Feberuary

10, 2013. http://peoplesworld.org/united-states-adds-
   bases-in-south-america/.

"Who's Afraid of Huawei?" *The Economist.* August 4, 2012.
   Accessed January 21, 2013.
   http://www.economist.com/node/21559922.

Wohlsen, Marcus. 2012. "Spies or No Spies, U.S. Companies
   Should Fear Huawei." *Wired.* October 8. Accessed
   January 21, 2013.
   http://www.wired.com/business/2012/10/spies-or-no-
   spies-u-s-companies-should-fear-huawei/.

www.ingramcontent.com/pod-product-compliance
Lightning Source LLC
Chambersburg PA
CBHW080438290526
45791CB00008BA/2550